Other M. Rubio's works:

Technical English Basics:

- ✓ Motorcycle, Tools and Safety (Book 1)

- ✓ Motorcycle, Basic Components (Book 2)

- ✓ Motorcycle, Engines (Book 3)

Novels and Tales:

- ✓ Her Angels and Demons

- ✓ Try the "YES", "NO" you have already

- ✓ No way, no discussion

- ✓ Orion

- ✓ Again

- ✓ Innocence

- ✓ Catalonia! Yes Sir!

- ✓ The diamond shoes

- ✓ The Fifth Amendment

- ✓ INTERVIEW: Pandemic and Immigrant. A brief report.

Amazon.com

SECRETARY / ASSISTANT

ORGANIZATION, PERFORMANCE AND CHARACTERISTICS

Practical Course

Book 1

M. Rubio

SECRETARY OR ASSISTANT

The companies key positions need to count with qualified personnel to provide them with necessary support for their organization and planning activities.

The under development projects daily management and their execution may depend, in order to achieve the objectives in time and quality, on the support they may receive.

It's in this organization and planning that the figure of the Secretary or, if you prefer, the Assistant, appears.

For the presented here work, I'd decided, due to a personal preference, to identify the professional as Secretary.

WHAT ABOUT COFFEE?

Here a "little brake", about the discussion that, in recent years, has been generated around the profession.

Out of pure prejudice, I hear a lot of people saying that they don't want to be named Secretary, since they don't admit including "serving coffee" in their functions.

As if "serving coffee" would be the only activity of a Secretary.

The Secretary profession is one of the most diversified you can imagine.

In reality, it unifies a series of activities, an endless number of responsibilities.

If you prefer not to serve coffee at a meeting and your company doesn't have the staff to do so, prepare the "coffee table" and leave everything at hand, so that the participants can help themselves.

You may be surprised to find that an executive has no problem serving own coffee, and receiving a lot of praise, after all, the meetings will, this way, happen without interruptions.

DIVERSITY

Diversity is the "magic word" that defines this profession.

How diverse can it be?

How much imagination can achieve.

As far as we can find different companies, with different departments.

It doesn't matter if it's a family business or a multinational.

The Secretary will always be needed.

PERFORMANCE

The agility and the organization smooth running will depend on your ability to assume responsibilities and your preparation, your knowledge.

Therefore, it's very important that you have the specific preparation to perform administrative tasks, organizing meetings, telephone assistance, agenda control, organizing events, etc.

Prepare yourself with the necessary technical knowledge.

THE COMPANY AND THE SECRETARY

It's undeniable the importance of the Secretary in the Organization for the agility in good results of each company.

You've studied and acquired the technical knowledge to carry out all the activities that concern you.

But don't forget to study and learn about your Company's activities.

You don't have to be an engineer to work with them.

Not even being a lawyer or a mechanic, you are a secretary.

However, it is very important you to be interested in knowing and understanding your Company.

What is it dedicated to?

What are the goals of the Company you work for?

What are the customers?

Which suppliers?

What's your Company's policy?

That and many other information, currently, can be found in a matter of minutes, over the Internet.

It's not necessary you to be already working with them.

These are checkings that can already be done by you when applying for that vacancy.

In the first interviews phase, you will generally not know what the company is, your contact will be with the external selector.

In this phase, will be valued your technical knowledge, which companies you have already worked for, the reasons that led you to change jobs, or professions.

Next phase, you will already know which company is requesting the professional, and that's when you cannot remain in complete ignorance.

All Company's official data are available on the Internet.

Study what they are engaged in, their financial situation, whether it's a family business or not.

If it's a multinational, check which countries are represented in.

All this information will help you in the interview outcoming, since, of course, they are looking for someone who can fit their needs.

But don't forget, when you're already there, to continue assimilating information.

Watch.

Study the policy of the Company you are working for.

*This will be the policy
you must comply with.*

Study their correspondence, reports, periodic meetings.

Study your co-workers behavior.

You can learn a lot from them.

Observe the person(s) you work with directly.

Only after knowing very well those people and the Company's needs, you will be able to put into practice some necessary changes, which the company is waiting you to make.

That's why they hired you.

That's the reason, they looked for a person with the necessary technical organizational knowledge.

But be careful!

Always respect the fact that, each person for or with whom you work, has the technical knowledge inherent to own role.

A Secretary should never compete with other functions, for "believing" outperforming them in knowledge.

And you should never, never, never compete with your boss.

Respect   *to*   *be* respected.

SHARED SECRETARY

With the companies current situation, it's increasingly common the secretary work to be shared.

Thus, in a commercial department, we'll have the secretary attending the Commercial Manager and its whole team.

We can see, very often, same secretary attending

the Commercial Director, the Financial Director and the Marketing Director.

This, if the General Director is not included.

And how can that be possible?

Isn't it excessive?

No.

We speak of the modern world, in which all companies, including "small" ones, already have computerized systems.

Almost each and every employee has his or her own computer terminal, whether connected to a network, or simply a "notebook".

So, this is the "great secret".

Every secretary must know very well how to use the facilities that information technology puts at their disposal.

A letter can be corrected in a matter of minutes, as can a report.

Charts can be prepared and corrected quickly, with the right tool.

Presentations can be ready in two hours time, just working on the slides, in order to reflect all the data, the results, and cause the necessary impact.

All of this, because you have the necessary technical knowledge to use the computer tools.

<u>Attention:</u>

You don't have to be a programmer or a systems analyst.

Rather, a "user" with the necessary technical knowledge.

However, remember that if your work is being shared by more than one board, by more than one department, it will be very important, for you not to generate a war within the Company, to be totally and absolutely **discreet**.

One board affairs should not be shared with another, by you.

For this, they hold meetings in which they discuss data, policies, objectives.

It's not your job to share information that had prematurely arrived in your hands.

Discretion is the most sought after quality in the secretary, and in this case it's fundamental.

It would be practically necessary for you to be a person when handling information from one board and another with the other.

Be sure that this is exactly what is expected of you.

THE SECRETARY AND THE CHARACTERISTICS THAT LEAD TO SUCCESS

In addition to technical knowledge and discretion, it's important to highlight some necessary characteristics for your profession.

<u>Good looking:</u>

It's not necessary to dress in designer clothes, to spend all your salary on clothing.

But choose what clothes to wear, shoes and accessories, every day.

Take a look in the mirror before leaving home and be honest with yourself when criticizing the result.

<u>Sympathy:</u>

Friendliness and good humor can also be learned.

Don't confuse "good humor" with "clowning" in your work environment.

Friendliness will open the way for the environment to become much lighter and more pleasant.

<u>Organization:</u>

Daily you have to deal with agendas, phone calls, documentation, meetings, and a lot of information that requires a huge organizational capacity.

An important technique to organize yourself daily is:

1) When arriving the Company, every day, make the agenda (s) review, check that all the necessary material for the meetings is prepared, if the rooms are available, make a general check to confirm that everything is in the right place, that the printer has sufficient paper, etc.

2) Review received correspondence, including emails, even if you would not to reply at that time.

It's important to know if, for example, the customer's presence had been canceled due to the delay in the flight's arrival.

3) Have a notebook available, to write down the date each day, the most important activities, the phone calls you must make, in short, to program yourself.

Also take note of the incoming calls and the reason for them.

Thus, you will have a "history" to consult, if necessary.

Don't just rely on your memory.

There's a lot of different information each day, a "history" will help.

Patience and skill with conflicts:

I often say that the secretary is the one "at the forefront of the battle", so it's almost certain to be "the first" to suffer the impacts.

Difficulties caused by delays in service time, frustrations due to shortcomings in the routine, customer dissatisfaction, are experiences that can become an enormous torment.

Patience and the ability to manage conflicts is essential for the situation not to get worse, and to control any installed confusion.

And remember:

1) The "I am like this" doesn't serve. You can change, re-educate yourself and get the patience needed to deal with all of these situations.

2) Customers are not just external.

As the link between your boss and everyone else in the company, the "catalyst element", your colleagues, in other departments, or even in your own department, must be considered and respected as customers.

They also depend on your good management.

Flexibility:

Despite working with fixed schedules, periodic meetings, repetitive activities, flexibility is an important feature.

A meeting can be extended beyond the scheduled time, for many reasons.

Or it may be necessary to start earlier "that" day, when the company is preparing to receive the customer, which can mean a contract, the financial "oxygen" of an entire year, with the reports and presentations that are fundamental to the desired success.

Understand, then, that some days the workday can start later and end later, as well as start earlier and end earlier.

It's important to understand that your flexibility is essential for everything to go smoothly, since you are a key player in the success of the environment.

Proactivity:

Proactive secretaries, in addition to being less dependent of their bosses approval to perform essential functions, help significantly improving the flow of routine operation, since they seek to solve problems independently, so that the professional can work smoothly.

But remember that your decisions must always be in line with your boss' work policy.

Good relationship:

Being able to maintain a good relationship with your boss, with coworkers, with customers and suppliers is essential for the environment to work without any problem.

These are the main characteristics for your success in this profession, but we could still mention a number of others, very important to maintain the much needed tranquility in the Company.

However, and intentionally left for our conversation ending, I believe that there are two characteristics that must always be present:

KINDNESS

AND

EMPATHY

Practice kindness and empathy in all areas of your work, especially when analyzing your colleagues activity.

THE SECRETARY AND THE IMPERATIVE TECHNICAL KNOWLEDGE

Although you should try to prepare yourself for the specific needs of the Company for which you work, there are some essential technical knowledge for the profession.

Here we list them, and they will be treated, in more detail, in the other books of the course:

- ✓ Computing
- ✓ Telephone attention
- ✓ Agenda's control
- ✓ Archive
- ✓ Administrative tasks
- ✓ Meetings Organization
- ✓ Travels organization
- ✓ Events organization
- ✓ Languages Knowledge

You'd taken the decision to prepare yourself for the profession that, for whatever reason, had been choosen by you.

Congratulations!

No matter the reasons that led to this choice.

In order to have the desired success, this preparation is essential.

Read, learn, observe, and always update your knowledge.

The world is evolving and all professionals must accompany this evolution, you too.

M. Rubio

www.ingramcontent.com/pod-product-compliance
Lightning Source LLC
Chambersburg PA
CBHW051354150726
48000CB00003B/1181